BIDEFORD
FIRE
BRIGADE

Ian Arnold

EDWARD GASKELL
The Lazarus Press
DEVON

Review Copy

DFRS.

With thanks,
Ian Arnold

BIDEFORD FIRE BRIGADE

British Library Cataloguing in Publication
A Catalogue record for this book is available from
the British Library

ISBN 1- 898546- 14- 2

Published
Typeset, Printed & Bound By
EDWARD GASKELL
The Lazarus Press
6 Grenville Street
Bideford Devon
EX39 2EA

ACKNOWLEDGEMENTS

Acknowledgements and thanks are also especially due to Pat Slade and her helpers at the Bideford Archive, Roy Cann, Peter Christie, Liz Shears, Joyce Webb and F.F. Alan Pearce and members of the Fire Brigade past and present who have so willingly given their assistance and reminiscences. Thanks must also go to Helen for the many hours spent typing and proof reading my original manuscript.

ADVANCE APOLOGY

Not much has been written about the fire brigade of Bideford before. One of the main reasons for this must be the lack of recorded factual information. For this reason it has been necessary for me to make assumptions now and again regarding dates and places of particular happenings. I would be very pleased to hear from anyone with corrections and facts or pictures regarding the Bideford Fire Brigade. Perhaps such information could be used in a future edition.

CONTENTS

ILLUSTRATIONS

(Between Pages 16 and 17)

INTRODUCTION

A hobby may be defined as a favourite subject or occupation that is not one's main business. My hobby is to collect medals of the first world war that were issued to people who lived in the North Devon area. Researching the "man behind the medal" can be a fascinating exercise and one that involves many other areas of study. Bringing a medal to life by finding out what the recipient did, where he lived and what he looked like involves an accumulated knowledge that has become popularly known as local history. It was a few years ago that I bought a group of four medals from a local man that included one issued by the National Fire Brigades Union for Long Service and Good Conduct. Although not a particularly rare combination the medals took pride of place in my collection since I was reliably informed that the recipient was a Bideford man.

Some time later I had the good fortune to obtain a group photograph of a fire brigade, and this too, I believed to be local and of the Bideford Fire Brigade (see illustration number 14). George Blackmore was the fireman to whom my medals belonged and he could have been any one of three firemen shown in the photograph – all were wearing the same combination of four medals.

My first job was to establish that my photograph was in fact that of the Bideford Fire Brigade, and then endeavour to identify each of the firemen on it. All my initial enquiries led me to Clifford Coates. Clifford is the undisputed "authority" on all matters relating to the fire brigade in Bideford and he was quickly able to confirm the names of many of the old-timers on my photograph, including my medal owner, 'Harry

Blackmore'. Such was his knowledge that I soon came to the conclusion that what he was able to relate could well be of use to others who are interested in local history and matters appertaining to the fire brigade.

Clifford Coates was originally from Lancashire and he moved to Bideford in 1948. An ex-Commando of the Royal Marines Clifford saw service in Sicily and Italy during the war and was present at the D day landings. At Salerno he was wounded in action and was later discharged from the Service in 1947. Together with his wife Evelyn he then spent most of his life building up the well known upholstery business in Bideford of, "C-Coates", in Lower Meddon Street. Sadly much of these premises were destroyed by fire in 1986 together with an old fire engine that Clifford owned. An ex Mayor, Town Councillor and Chairman of the Bideford Bridge Trust, Clifford joined the Fire Brigade in 1954. He became Station Officer in 1970 and retired from the service in 1979. A total of twenty five years with Station 4, Bideford, Devon Fire Brigade. From the medals, to the photograph, and with Clifford's inspiration and help I made further researches and contacts and gradually gathered sufficient information to put this little book together.

Ian Arnold. Bideford, December 1995.

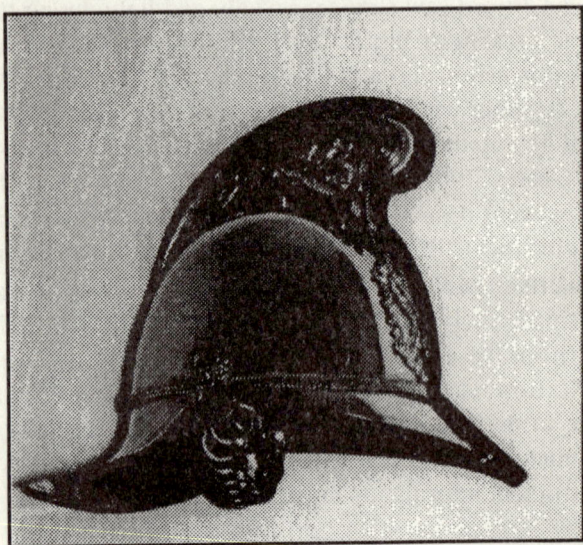

The silver helmet once worn by Harry Blackmore. He and Captain Charles Morris wore silver while the men wore the standard issue in brass.

1. The Early Years

The earliest reference made to fire prevention measures in Bideford appears to have been made in the year 1631 when furze, a kind of gorse, was forbidden to be stacked outside buildings or next to pottery kilns. Furze burns very rapidly and it was often used in the glazing process of pottery. The order was made following a fire that was recorded by the Corporation as being an 'awful and lamentable experience'. Nearly thirty years later a local benefactor donated twelve water buckets to the town for the use of the inhabitants in the event of a fire. Oddly enough over the next two hundred and fifty years buckets featured rather strongly in the minutes of fire committee meetings. In 1903 the Borough Council came in for some very severe criticism when it, too, bought a dozen new buckets for the use of the fire brigade. In those early days though, there was no fire brigade. As a fire fighting measure some people at certain points around the town were required to put barrels of water outside their houses or shops ready for use in a fire.

According to Alison Grant and Peter Christie, (*The Book of Bideford*), the first fire fighting appliance in Bideford was provided by the Bridge Trust in 1770. In September of 1769 the Steward of the Trust was instructed to write a letter to London to enquire the price of the best constructed engine. What the actual cost was is not recorded but the Bridge Trust paid £50 and the rest was raised by public subscription. It was probably a manually pulled and operated pump with a length of leather hose. For many years the fire "Station" was located beneath the Town Hall, which was where the present Council

Offices are. Special shelving had to be put up in the cellar for the storage of the leather hose. Every two months or so the engine was taken out and tested or, "played off" as it was put then. Mr George Heard was in charge. The rooms beneath the Town Hall were also used as the Police Station in those days and then, as now, the work required of the policeman and that of the fireman was fairly common. In those early years it was expected that the police, and anyone else for that matter, who arrived early at the scene of a fire, would do their best to lend a hand to put it out. Nevertheless, much property was lost and it was proved time and time again that adequate insurance cover was essential. It was actually the fire insurance companies who set up the first fire brigades as we know them, employing and training an emergency team of fire fighters. They provided their men with the latest fire fighting appliances and equipment and with this knowledge and equipment the firemen did their best to save the lives and property of the people who were insured with their company. In large cities there was often very fierce competition between the insurance companies and their rival fire brigades. In nineteenth century Bideford though, it was only the West of England Insurance Company that boasted its own Fire Brigade and engine. They attended and fought fires locally whether the unfortunate victims were insured with their parent company or not. No doubt compensation and expenses were claimed from the appropriate persons later. Only the Bideford Town Fire Brigade (at the times when there was one) provided any com-

petition for the West of England Brigade. Both the Town and
the West of England engines were pulled by horses and both
were manned by keen volunteers. These volunteers were paid a
retainer, much the same as is done today. Before steam was
introduced to raise the pressure the pumps were manually operated. Two teams of men stood either side of the 'engine', and
they pumped for all they were worth!

Delivery of the New Fire Engine
According to an account given in the North Devon Journal, the
delivery of a new fire engine to the Bideford branch of the West
of England Insurance Company in 1847 was filled with excite-
ment and drama. The engine was hand crafted in polished
mahogany and was of the very latest design being mounted as it
was on a fully sprung chassis. It had been built by "Kingdons"
of Exeter and they were the major ironmongers and iron-
founders in the whole of the West of England at that time. The
engine was pulled by four horses and when delivery was due a
crew of firemen was sent from Bideford to Exeter to fetch it. A
number of the "top brass" from both the West of England
Insurance Company and from Kingdons were invited to be present at the official handing-over ceremony. Everyone was
looking forward to witnessing the power of the new machine.
The representatives and honoured guests made their journey to
Bideford on board the regular coach which was named the
"Hero". The "Hero" left Exeter not long after the engine, and it
was a peaceful enough journey for most of the way until just a
couple of miles outside of Bideford. Somewhere along the
road from Torrington the coach caught up with the fire engine.
No doubt encouraged by certain of the occupants of his
coach, the coachman decided to try and overtake the West of
England Brigade and thus make their entry into Bideford first.

The fire engine driver was having none of this though, and
as the laden passenger coach pulled out, the Captain of the
brigade spurred his four-in-hand team into action. The race
was on! Both teams of horses were whipped to full speed for

the last sprint home along the Alverdiscott Road. Eight galloping horses, two carriages and narrow country lanes approaching Bideford, an accident was almost bound to happen. As the fire engine pulled away, it was the passenger coach that lost the road. Mr Anstey of Kingdons was outside riding on the box. He was pitched clean off of it and landed in a thorn bush. He was injured quite seriously with a gash to his face. Another passenger, a gentleman from London, was thrown fifteen feet over a hedge. The coach itself was wrecked. Parts of it were strewn for many yards along the Alverdiscott Road. Hearing the crash behind them and seeing the plight of their friends the fire brigade turned around to perform their first rescue with the new engine. Whether the handing over ceremony ever took place after this little incident is not actually recorded, but no doubt there were some pretty sharp words exchanged somewhere along the line.

When an alarm was raised, then as now, the first priority was to get the men and engine to the fire. After that, of course, there was the essential need of water. Fire engines at this time were filled with water by buckets passed from hand to hand or by pipes that were laid to it from any convenient source. The limited power of the jet meant that the engine had to be taken very close in to the fire. It was a real possibility that the fire engine itself could catch on fire! Bideford in the mid nineteenth century had two appliances and two fire crews protecting its population of under 6000. The rivalry between the fire brigades can be judged from a newspaper report of November

4

1851 in which Mr Hamlyn, of the West of England Brigade, is accused of refusing to loan his spare buckets to the Town Brigade at the scene of a fire. The North Devon Journal reports that, "if he had lent his buckets as requested the fire would have been put out in five minutes". At this time engines without the proper supply of buckets were useless. When the Council next met they authorised the Fire Engine Committee to purchase 24 buckets, one dozen at 12 shillings each, and one dozen at 8 shillings and 6 pence each. It was suggested that these be attached to the engine so that they were taken out with it automatically. No doubt the authorities may have thought themselves well-off for fire protection at this time, but from the account of a fire reported by the Bideford Gazette of 15 December 1857, this does not appear to be the case. The fire was at Southcott Farm, Westleigh.

TREMENDOUS FIRE

On Thursday at 1 o'clock, PM fire broke out at the Farmhouse "Southcott", which is about a mile and a half from Bideford, lying direct east, and occupied by Mr Thomas Brayley. As soon as the fire was discovered no time was lost in dispatching the West of England engine, under the superintendence of Mr E M White, and the Town engine under the superintendence of Mr Wm. Major. The later being the first on the spot was immediately put to work, and in about ten minutes from this time the West of England and the Town engine were working side by side. Hundreds hastened to the conflagration and many lent a willing hand in supplying the engines with water, which was plentiful, but the flames had got such an ascendancy, that at length the working of the engines was directed against the outbuildings and the adjacent cottages, to prevent the further spread of the fire. Every part of the dwelling-house, sheep pens, dairy, wash house, and stables are destroyed. Every part was covered in thatch, and when this fell in, the flames and the crash were terrible.

The report goes on to state that the cottage was over 300 years old and that the cause was probably a servant-girl who accidentally dropped some hot charcoal on the stairs. Charcoal was used to scald milk and such practices together with the use of candles and oil lamps, open fires and gas lamps, made it a wonder that there were not far more fires than there actually were. Great care was needed and careless persons faced prosecution. As late as 1923 a one David Satterthwaite was fined two shillings and sixpence for allowing his chimney to be on fire in Mill Street. Sparks and ash was falling into the road and onto the roofs of the adjoining properties.

Two Brigades

As already explained for much of the nineteenth century Bideford had two fire brigades. One was managed by the Town authorities and the other by the West of England Insurance Company. By 1860 the Town Brigade had two appliances of its own and in December of that year they were tested in a competition arranged with the West of England Brigade. Between them the firemen worked the three engines and they played their hoses over the Town Hall. Mr Major led the Town Brigade, and the jets, it was observed, showed a remarkable power of propulsion. Mr Way directed the West of England team. The Gazette reporter of the event noted that while the volume of water from the West of England hose seemed greater, it did not throw so far. The whole exercise didn't last very long though. After a short while one of the hoses of the Town Brigade burst and then the other two appliances ceased to function because the water ran out! It is hard to understand how this could have happened with the river so close at hand, but perhaps the tide was out and nobody fancied getting wet.

Checking the apparatus and practising the crew by way of a competition was repeated a couple of years later in 1862. This time, the engine of the Insurance Company had undergone reconditioning in Exeter and no doubt the West of England brigade wanted to show it off and "get their own back" on the Town Brigade. Their engine was in fine order. They were able to squirt water clear over the top of the flag-pole on the roof of the Town Hall. Apparently it was now the turn of the town engine to look feeble by comparison. These competitions were always undertaken in good heart though, and this was usually proved by everyone involved going to the local pub afterwards. The Town Brigade in this year, 1862, was made up of E Major, A Cawsey, J Fulford, T Crossman, J Lile, W Burnard, P Bower, W Williams, W West, J Elliot, H Prouse and J Berry. They were each paid ten shillings per year, £6 being put aside by the Council for the purpose! In these years the competitions and celebrations were undertaken on a regular basis. One year it was Tantons Hotel that was to get a thorough washing down. In 1868 a whole procession attached themselves behind the brigades as they made their way to Westward Ho! for their annual dinner. The West of England engine must have looked majestic as it was drawn by four fine horses driven by two postillions in blue and white livery. Music was provided by a band of wondering minstrels. Everyone enjoyed a celebration in those days, and no doubt a jolly good time was had by one and all. Except for the few who, hopefully, were left in the town to deal with any emergency!

In 1866 Hyfield House burned down. It was a house of some significance and the home of Doctor Thomas Pridham who was a popular local surgeon. Both brigades attended the fire as did hundreds of local people, "of all social classes" who worked feverishly to dowse the flames. Although much of the contents of the house were saved the upper parts of the thatched building had to be demolished. It was rebuilt however and is now called 'Iffield', the home of artist Reg Lloyd.

By 1870 it was reported in a council meeting that the Town engine had fallen into a bad state of repair. Its condition was not improved one councillor observed, by the loaning of it to private individuals so that they could pump sea water out of their boats! "Staunching" of vessels in this way was actually practised for quite a number of years. It brought some useful income to the council when they started charging seven shillings and sixpence per time.

It was in the 1870s that the Town was provided with its first "fire-plugs" or hydrants for the connection of hose pipes to the mains. This greatly increased the fire fighting efficiency of the brigades, but unfortunately the water supply itself was not always very reliable. Indeed in 1891, before the second Gammaton Reservoir was built, the council narrowly defeated a motion to turn the water supply off at night. This practice, shutting off the water in times of shortage, was a major factor in the loss of Edgehill College some thirty years later, and this, even after a similar decision had contributed to the loss of a major part of Ilfracombe town centre in the "Ilfracombe Great Fire" of 1896.

Sometime in the 1870s and 1880s it appears that the Bideford Town Fire Brigade as a unit, was disbanded. Perhaps it was felt that the expense of their upkeep was no longer justified now that there were hydrants around the town. In any case a lot of money needed to be spent on the engine and on replacement equipment. In 1876 the West of England fire engine was reconditioned at W & J Abbots foundry at considerable cost and new pipes had to be added with connections that would fit the new water hydrants. The fighting of fires in Bideford now reverted to the cover of the West of England Brigade for some time. In an emergency the Town apparatus was operated by the police, or by council officials and volunteers. It was Mr Chipman for example, the Superintendent of Police, who had to arrange for the Town engine to attend a fire in 1882.

2. The Return of the Brigade

The industrial revolution and the expansion of the railway as a means of communication changed the lives of everyone in Britain. Bideford was no exception and when the railway arrived in 1856 the area maintained considerable growth until the end of the nineteenth century. With more private and commercial property there was an increasing need for the formation of a properly trained fire brigade once more. The "Bideford Gazette" was firmly of this opinion, as was made clear in its editorial columns on a number of occasions. In February of 1885 the call was repeated in a comment saying that while the West of England Brigade was still providing a very fine service, it was just not enough. The Town by now had plenty of appliances and they were in good working condition, but there were no men who were actually trained in how to use and set up the equipment. In short there was no Town Fire Brigade in existence and there ought to be. The point was forcefully brought home just a month later, when two major fires rocked the area in one week. The first was at Horwood House, the home of the Reverend John Dene, when a number of outhouses were destroyed. The second was at App's Brewery, Littleham. App's beer and mineral waters were known far and wide across North Devon and the brewery was a major employer in the area. The fire there was a considerable disaster. In fact the brewery had been taken over a little earlier and was at the time owned by Phillbrick, but it was still popularly known by local people as "App's Brewery". The fire broke out on a quiet Sunday morning and it was devastating in its effect. Once more

9

the word quickly spread through the town that a big fire was in progress and literally hundreds of people from the district raced to the scene to watch. In these days when the fire engine bell was heard, townsfolk literally dropped everything to be a part of the action. The attitude of people can be judged by the newspaper reporter who commented, "Had the outbreak occurred at night the scene would have been one of exceptional grandeur; as it was it was sufficiently impressive and exciting". Sometimes the firemen would shout their intended destination from the galloping engine as it sped towards the fire. That way they could be sure of some willing hands for fetching water. Hundreds made it to Littleham that day. And hundreds more, who for one reason or another missed the actual spectacle, went later, to see its aftermath. The population of Bideford it would appear took the fire at a brewery to be a most serious affair! The fire was discovered about 9.30 in the morning. It was recorded in the newspaper report that it took a messenger twenty minutes to reach Bideford and to raise the alarm. It then took a further ten minutes or so to get the men together, to get the fire engine out of its store on the Quay and to fetch the horses.

The horses had to be taken from the New Inn Stables by the Market down to the Fire Station on the Quay where they were then hitched to the engine before the race to the fire could finally be made. No time was wasted and App's Brewery was reached in about another half an hour. Not bad going for Superintendent John Abbott, Captain Way and the men of the West of England Brigade. But a lot can happen to buildings that are on fire within an hour. Especially grouped as these were in two sides of a triangle. Some of the buildings were three stories high. In the course of the day as the fire raged the main buildings were completely gutted. In the face of such an inferno the Brigade and their engine had little real effect. They did make some difference though and their efforts were not entirely in vain.

Through their hard work, a new and expensive boiler in an adjoining outbuilding was saved and so, too, was a large quantity of beer that was stored in the cellar. Perhaps the firemen and their helpers worked especially hard to save this valuable commodity!

An Extra £2 Per Year
There now followed various suggestions and proposals regarding the setting up of a new Fire Brigade. As is so often the case, it took a major incident for the need to be realised. Even so it was not until 1886, a year later, that a positive decision was made by the "Local Board" to set up a volunteer Fire Brigade. The first thing they had to do was to appoint a suitable captain. The job was offered to Mr Morgan the Superintendent of Police with an extra £2 per year on his pay. Not much to set up and train the proposed twelve-man Brigade. Mr Morgan didn't think so either, which he made plain in a letter to the council turning down their offer. He didn't want the added responsibility anyway, as Chief of the Bideford Police he felt he had enough to do. Thus it was nearly two years after the App's Brewery fire before the Bideford Gazette was finally able to report in February of 1887:

THE FIRE BRIGADE THAT IS TO BE.

The Committee reported that they had directed a Fire Brigade to be formed to consist of ten men and a captain; the men to be paid £1 per annum for attendance at drills; the captain to be paid £3. The Borough Surveyor had been appointed captain, and it was understood that the men should find their own clothes. The Surveyor had been directed to order the necessary belts and axes, and other appliances, and had been instructed to proceed without delay with the formation of the Brigade.

An additional payment was agreed to be made to the men for their attendance at fires.

The earliest known photograph of the Bideford Fire Brigade was first published in *The Book of Bideford* by Alison Grant and Peter Christie. It belongs to the North Devon

Museum Trust and is reproduced within our illustration pages by permission. Taken about 1890 it shows the full crew of ten men with their smart new uniforms and flat pill-box caps with the letters BFB – Bideford Fire Brigade. As the newspaper report mentioned, the men had to provide their own uniform. This practice was continued right up until 1915. In those days the uniforms were used for ceremonial purposes only and no doubt the firemen found them far too expensive to wear anywhere near a fire! The Captain of the Brigade, (centre), is Henry Chowins. He was the Borough Surveyor and he lived at number 3 River View Terrace. Later he moved to number 6 Cooper Street and this was closer to the fire station which was at this time on the Broad Quay. As Captain of the Fire Brigade Henry Chowins was the keeper of the keys to the Fire Brigade Station. It would appear that the Town had now taken over the West of England Brigade premises and equipment or, more likely, there was an amalgamation of the two. As well as Henry Chowins the photograph shows fireman Hearn holding the hydrant key in the front row. His son, Joseph Hearn is seen second from the right (illustration number 6) in the 1926 picture while his grandson, Kingsley Hearn, is on the left of the 1959 picture. (illustration number 26) Thus there were three generations of the Hearn family in the Bideford fire service spanning nearly one hundred years.

As previously explained, Bideford by this time had a piped water supply with hydrants fitted

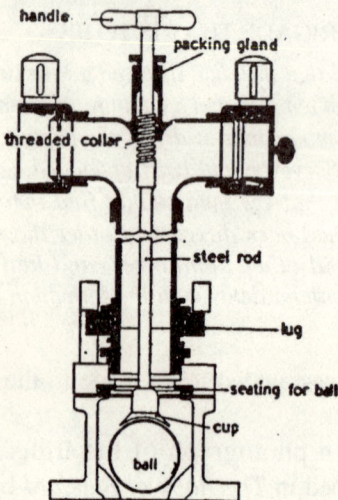

Standpipe: ball type, with lug connection.

12

in the mains at various points around the town. Before a hose can be connected to the water supply, a standpipe is connected to the hydrant. A screw-down ball type standpipe is seen held by the fireman to the left of Henry Chowins. This was fitted to the mains by a bayonet socket arrangement, then the brass handle (seen at the top) was wound down to depress a ball in the hydrant, so releasing the water. The hose was connected to the standpipe at the connection by the fireman's hand and the right-hand fireman holds the branch pipe and nozzle ready for connection to the hose. The last ball type hydrant in existence in Bideford that this equipment would fit is in the sports ground.

The Fire Bell
In the event of a fire the alarm was raised by the ringing of the bell in the tower above the Police Station in the Town Hall. The octagonal tower is still there and can be seen on the north west corner of the building. The sounding of this bell though, was not a very satisfactory arrangement. For one thing it was not always possible to get at its rope to sound it. For another, it was not loud enough. According to a Bideford Gazette newspaper correspondent of the day, when the bell was rung in an emergency, it sounded more like a child's toy than an alarm bell! Added to this, it was unreliable. When it was needed to call out the new Fire Brigade to their first really big fire in 1891, it would not work at all. Two policemen pulled enthusiastically on its rope for some time but it made no sound. It was just after one o'clock on a cold February morning and Kivells' Coachbuilding Works at the end of Mill Street was well ablaze. The bell was useless. The alarm was finally raised and the firemen alerted by Mr Martin who shouted from his horse-back as he galloped around the streets of the town.

By the time the Brigade arrived there were a number of people attempting to fight the fire as best they could. Foremost among these was a desperate householder who was pouring water over the roof of his cottage from buckets passed up to him by the crowd. Evidently this "do it yourself" fire fighter was not very patient nor very complimentary toward the Fire Brigade when they arrived. He thought they should have been somewhat quicker and he told them so. While the firemen rushed around connecting their standpipe and hose he was shouting abuse from the rooftop. Captain Chowins and his men were not to be ruffled though. Calmly they connected their gear and responded by blasting a cold jet of water directly over him! The pressure was good and he was knocked clean off his perch.

Two hoses were quickly put to work and there was a good supply of water. After a while the blaze was fully extinguished but not before Kivell's was extensively damaged. The whole workshop and eleven or twelve coaches were completely destroyed. The fire was particularly intense because as well as all the wood, there were considerable quantities of flammable liquids such as paint and varnish in the workshops. The intensity of the blaze can be judged by the fact that glass was melted in the building and some of the furniture in nearby houses was too hot to handle for it to be taken out into the street for safety. The efficiency of the new Brigade was proved that night as they contained a fire which otherwise could have spread rapidly through the densely populated areas of Mill Street and Coldharbour. Many of the townspeople of Bideford had now witnessed the turnout of their new Fire Brigade and most were very pleased with what they had seen.

3. The Twentieth Century

Frederick Lee of Wellbrook Terrace replaced Henry Chowins as the Captain of the Bideford Brigade for much of the first part of the twentieth century. The keys to the station were now kept at number 2 Allhalland Street. For a time, the stand-pipes, branches and the other equipment necessary was carried on a hand-cart that was rushed from its store on the Quay. Pushing any sort of hand-cart around the streets of Bideford is no easy matter and the men must have been pretty fit to run to a fire with the cart and then set up the gear and fight the fire. A second hand-cart and its associated equipment was kept in the Market Place, but at many council meetings there was lively debate as to whether this was sufficient. In 1903 Alderman Dymond the chairman of the Fire Brigade Committee reported that he thought it was. When it was revealed that the council had recently bought twenty-four new buckets for the use of the Brigade there was uproar! A number of councillors thought that what was needed was a modern fire engine, not buckets. The argument was that it was not just the cost of buying a new fire engine but the added cost of looking after it – that was the problem. The purchase and up-keep of a steam fire engine would be a considerable burden on the rates. In any case the Town had ample provision of fire plugs.

The equipment stored in the Quay Station at this time included: one hand-cart, 300 feet of hose, one nozzle, one standpipe, five wrenches, one water key, one boat-hook, one set of blocks and tackle, one canvas basket, one "jumping sheet", six belts, six axes, one ladder and of course, twelve new buckets. The rest of the buckets and a similar list of equipment

1

The earliest known picture of Bideford Fire Brigade, about 1890.

Centre: Captain Henry Chowins

Back Row: left to right Firemen Lloyd, Champion, (Unknown), Shortridge, Glover.

Front Row: left to right Firemen Lee, Unknown, Hearn, and Babb.

(North Devon Museum Trust)

2

A Victorian photograph showing the brigade leading
the new Mayor out of St Mary's Church to his
Chambers. The 'X' is at the foot of Fireman Backway.

3

A Classic picture of the Torrington Fire Brigade in
front of their Merryweather horse-drawn appliance
in 1907.
Unfortunately I have not been able to locate a similar one of the Bideford Brigade but this is included
for comparison. The Captain was Alderman T.W.
Heywood but who is the lad on the right?

4

Another photograph taken near Torrington, this time after a
fire at Woodhouse Farm, May 1907. In those days a fire
attracted a goodly number of onlookers and potential helpers.
This charming study shows a typical cross section of the local
community, many of them enjoying a cup of tea after their toil.

5

Town Crier Sidney 'Taggy' Braund leads the fire brigade up
Meddon Street in a Civic procession to mark the opening of
Bideford's new hospital, September 1925.

The Fire at Woodbury Mill...

6

The Brigade, 'On Parade' for the passing of the new Mayor on his way to Chambers, 1926. Many were still serving about twelve years later when photograph number 14 was taken. From the left is Charles Morris, Tommy Sherbourne, Harry Cole, Joe Glover, George 'Harry' Blackmore, Reggie Prance, William Sherbourne, Bill Shute, Bill Dennis, George Hearn, Bill Blackmore, Tommy Gorrel and Ernie Dunn.

(Permission Stn. O. Graham Tucker).

7

Charles Kingsley looks onto the arrival of Bideford's first motor fire engine the celebrated 'Grenville', June 5th 1927. Councillors Harry Hopson and Dr E J Toye are on board. Beside Frank Passmore, the driver, is the Mayor, Alderman J. M. Metherell J.P., C. A.

(Liz Shears)

8

Bideford, Northam and District Joint Fire Committee at the opening of the New Fire Station, Old Town, Bideford, 21 December 1928. Chairman W.T. Goaman stands on the side-board with Chief Officer Charles Morris at the wheel of the 'Grenville'.

(Permission Stn.O.,Graham Tucker)

9

The 'Grenville' once more, this time at the head of the funeral procession of Fireman William P. Sherbourne, 26 November 1932. Fireman Sherbourne had served twelve years with the Bideford Brigade and died at the early age of 47. He was a painter and decorator by trade.

Members of the Brigade who attended the funeral: Chief Officer C. Morris, Second Officer G. Blackmore, Engineer E. Radshaw, Firemen W. Blackmore, T. Gorrill, W. Shute, W. Dennis, S. Morris, E. Dunn, J. Glover and H. Moore.

10

The complete devastation of Grenville College is apparent from this photograph taken the morning after the fire.

11

These groundsmen and staff helped the firemen tackle the Grenville College blaze with a handcart and buckets of water from a well. At one stage it was proposed to send to Barnstaple for their steam fire engine, but without water it was decided there was little point.

(Alan Pearce)

12 & 13

Two Picrures taken in the Sports Ground when Bideford hosted the National Fire Brigades Association Regional Competitions in 1935. About 200 firemen took part from nineteen South Westwern brigades. The top photograph shows the Mayor, Councillor W.E. Ellis, making his welcoming address. The bottom photograph shows the presentation of the Hobbs Memorial Shield (bestowed in honour of the late Chief Officer of the Yeovil Brigade). Bideford, conspicuous in their shining brass helmets, won two of the ten trophies.

(Steve Saunders)

14

The photograph that started it all! Bideford Fire Brigade displaying their cups and shields about 1938. Pictured from left to right:

Back row: Tommy Sherbourne. Joe Glover. Stan Morris (son of Charles). Harry Moore. Bill dennis. Frank Cole. Jack Mallett.

Front row: Bill Nicholls. Reggie Prance (Engineer). Chief Officer Charles Morris. George 'Harry' Blackmore (2 I. C.) and Bill Blackmore (brother of George).

Harry Moore and Frank Cole are still alive and well today, and living in Bideford.

15

The 'Grenville' and crew on manoeuvres along the Westleigh Straight before the war. George Blackmore was in command. Note the wicker baskets on the escape ladder which were used as water strainers.

(Clifford Coates)

16

An early wartime photograph taken outside the Bideford Fire Station. Standing in the rain around the Godiva Centrifugal Major Pump are Company Officer Charles Morris with retained "regular' firemen Frank Passmore and Stan Morris flanked by AFS firemen Joe Potter and Trevor Green.

(Paula Martin)

17

This photograph shows the war-time strength of Bideford fire Brigade which included seven ladies. Rhona Hearn is fourth from the right in the middle row. Officer Pat White, Firewomen Nancy Harris and May Winsburgh are 7th, 8th and 9th respectively in the front row. The picture was posed outside the NFS station, East-the-Water.

(Clifford Coates)

18 & 19

The unique Bideford Fire Barge, 'Good Hope' at her moorings. Leading Fireman Arthur Pridham is at the controls. The 'Good Hope' was the only jet-propelled fire barge belonging to the National Fire Service. Arthur Pridham, together with some local helpers, was instrumental in her development. Before her conversion to a fire barge the 'Good Hope' was the Ilfracombe Lifeboat.

(Liz Shears)

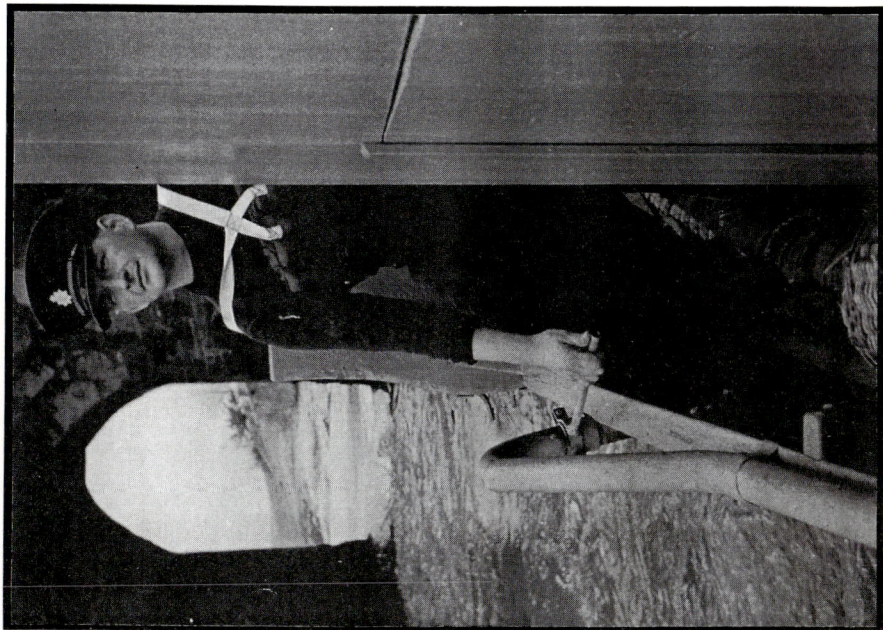

20 & 21

Two wartime photographs, locations unknown. Some familiar faces
in the top one are Kingsley Hearn, left, next to him is Arthur Pridham.
Among those seated are Bert Hilson, Wilfy Beckley and Arthur
Upton. The lower picture shows the crew in anti-gas protective clothing with George Blackmore on the right.

(Liz Shears)

22

An unusual night-time photograph taken by Knights of Barnstaple. Bideford's
fire engine the 'Grenville' is at work on what is probably Sidney House fire in
Torrington, 1942.
Bill Nicholls is lit by the acetylene lamps of the engine while a Torrington man
looks on.

(Ian Arnold)

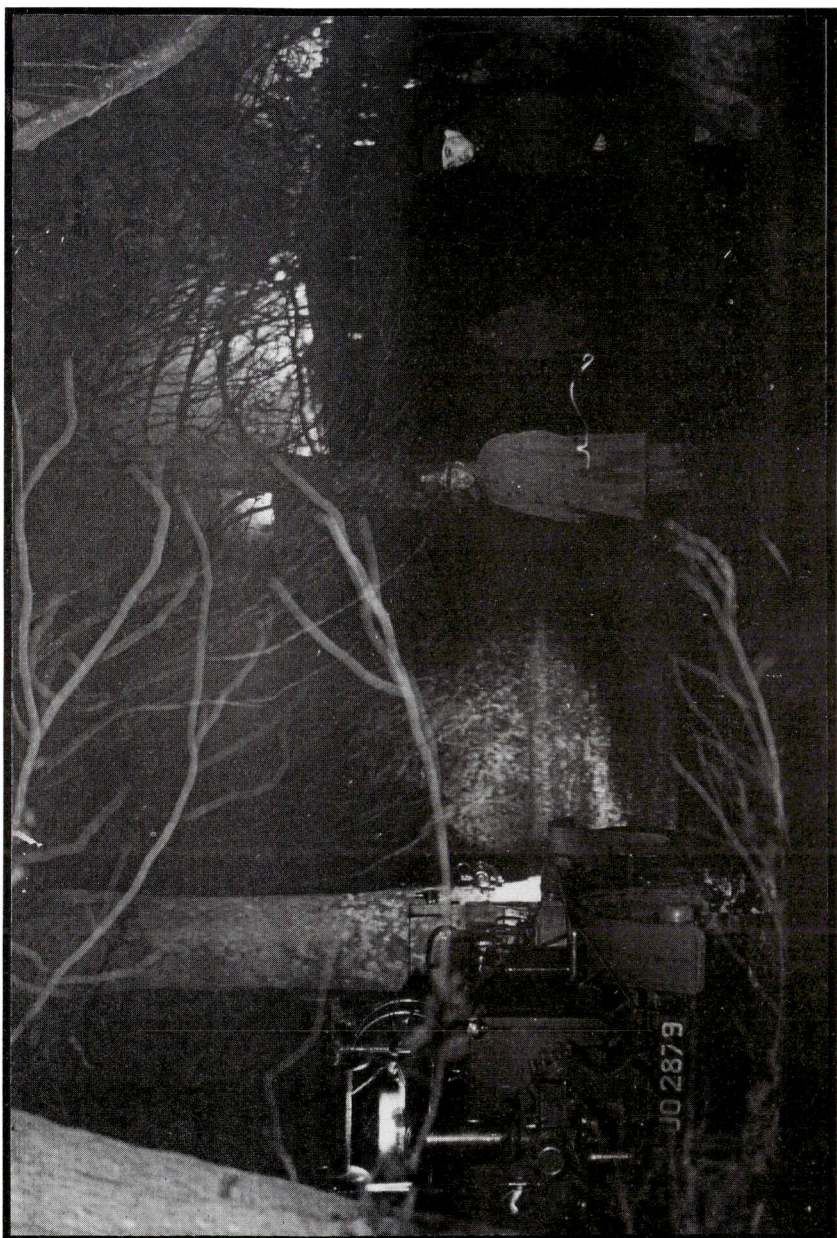

23

Post War appliances and crew getting ready for the carnival procession in Avon Road, East-the-Water. In addition to those named below, the top photograph shows Frank Passmore on the right.

24

On top of the engine : Arthur Upton, (next to him – unknown).
Left to right : Tom Trick, Jack Botting, Frank Cole, Jack Heywood.
C.O. Fred Tithecott, Albert Short, Les Buckley.

(Clifford Coates)

25

Fire crew children and their friends aboard the 'Kipling' in the Coronation year of 1953. Waving from the front wing is David Webb now a full-time fireman in Exeter. He is the son of Reginald 'Ted' Webb, a Bideford fireman for 27 years before his untimely death in 1952. Others to be spotted include Kingsley Hearn's daughter; Ivor Giddy's two sons; Fred Tithecot's son; Tom Trick's daughter; Jack Haywood's son and daughter, and so on!

(Clifford Coates)

26

Devon County Fire Service, Station 'B' 9, Bideford 1959.
Back row: Fm. Ted Webb, Ivor Shortridge, Reg Balls, Ron Hammett.
Middle row: Fm. Louis Rowson, Tom Glover, Ivor Giddy, Clifford Coates, Louis Violet, Graham Cole, Jack Heywood, Alan Percicole.
Front Row: L. Fm. Kingsley Hearn, S.O. Tom Trick, Stn. O. Fred Tithecott, L. Fm. Bill Nicholls, Fm. Jack Mallett.

(Clifford Coates)

27

Devon County Fire Brigade, Station 4, Bideford. The occasion is Station Officer Clifford Coates' retirement in 1979. No fewer than seven men in this photograph are still serving today.

They are back row : FF Alan Pearce (3rd left). FF Alan Branch, (5th left). LFF Michael Oliver (7th left). Sub/O Les Martin (9th left). Stn/O Graham Tucker (10th left).

Front row : Sub/O Dave Slade (1st left) and FF John Branch, (not pictured).

(Clifford Coates)

28

The latest Long Service Medals and Certificates were awarded in January 1995. Torridge District Officer Bob Prince presented medals to Sub Officers Les Martin and Dave Slade of Bideford and Sub Officer Dave Lawrence of Appledore.

(North Devon Gazette)

The current Long Service Medal bears the legend 'For Exemplary Fire Service' on the reverse. It was instituted in 1954 and is awarded to all ranks of local authority fire brigades, whether full or part-time, after twenty tears of exemplary service. The ribbon is red with yellow stripes

The 1995 Line-Up

Back Row : Geoff Violet, Alan Branch, Shane Martin, Stephen Hillman, Stn/O Graham Tucker, Jeff Utley, Jeff Harding, Andrew Blackwell, Neil Sanders.

Front Row : Bruce Lesslie, Trevor Lane, Robert Slade, Andrew Curtis, Brian Cole, Alan Pearce, John Branch, Michael Oliver.

Not in the picture are : Sub Officers Les Martin and Dave Slade.

Geoff Violet's father served in the Brigade and Robert Slade is the son of Dave. John and alan branch are brothers. As we say, 'the tradition continues!'

Photograph courtesy Brian P. Saunders

were stored in the Market Station. Alderman Dymond remind-
ed the council that added provision for fire fighting included
ladders and fire buckets which were fixed to the walls at various strategic positions around the Town. As well as at the fire
stations, ladders were provided at Old Town and East the Water
and there were more ladders available at the council yard,
although it was admitted that extra ladders should be provided
for the Mill Street and Strand areas of the Town.

The debate continued. It was all very well having all this
equipment but in addition to the men struggling to reach a fire
with a heavy hand-cart, when they got to the outskirts or to the
higher parts of the Town, the water pressure would be insufficient to be properly effective anyway. Even with the new
Higher Gammaton Reservoir now connected, the water would
only just reach the first floor of the highest houses in Westcroft.
In yet higher locations such as the Clovelly Road householders
complained of poor mains water pressure at the best of times.

The First Steam Engine

Although it does not appear to be reported in the newspaper, in
1917 the Town Council at last made the decision to purchase its
first steam fire engine. The Shand Mason steamer with glisten-
ing brass chimney was bought second-hand from Barnet Fire
Brigade in London. The purchase price was £225. It had a
quick-firing boiler which meant that sufficient steam for the
pump could be produced in just fifteen minutes. The paper,
sticks and coal were laid-in ready for firing in an emergency.
Sometimes after a fire, if there was any risk of it restarting, the
fire-box was kept stoked for a while so that the engine had
"steam up" in readiness. When up to its working pressure of
some 100 pound per square inch the pump was able to propel a
3/4 inch jet of water 75 feet. No longer were men needed to
power the pump when away from mains water. This appliance
was also housed in the Pannier Market building, in what is now
Honey's the butcher shop, on the corner of Butcher's Row. A
suitably central point for the despatch of the engine to any part

of the Town or surrounding country. The horses needed to pull the "steamer" were allowed to graze on the common land at Pollyfield, East the Water, and they were stabled at the New Inn in the Market Place. Later there were times when the "steamer" was pulled by a lorry although it must be remembered that there was strict control on the speed of vehicles at that time.

Edgehill College Fire

The inadequacy of this whole arrangement though, was perhaps nowhere better illustrated than by the fire that totally destroyed Edgehill College in June of 1920. This fire had all the ingredients for a major disaster. There were about 140 sleeping schoolgirls and staff in the building when the fire broke out in the early hours of the morning. Fortunately, once again, not one life was lost. The total loss of the building however, despite all the efforts of the fire-fighters, showed without doubt just what could have happened. For some reason only the hand-cart appears to have been used, but even this was useless when it was found that the water pressure was insufficient or even at some points, non existent. Owing to long standing water shortages in Bideford the school was being temporarily supplied from Northam and that council turned the water supply off at night. Even after the necessary valves had been operated to enable water to be got from the Bideford mains, the pressure was hopelessly poor. Perhaps the worst frustration to a fireman is to be at the scene of a fire without the essential supply of water. Frederick Lee and his men did all they could. In an effort to raise the pressure, water from the Gammaton Reservoir was diverted directly in to the mains, by-passing the normal filtering system. That raised the pressure all right, but so much so that it burst the main water pipe. The result was a total loss of mains water, not just to Edgehill College, but to the whole of Bideford. The firemen were not to blame. There was no delay in their turn out. The Captain and his nine crew members were at the scene within fifteen minutes together with their hand-cart and about 600 feet of hose and the ladder fire escape.

But all they and the Edgehill staff could do was to fight the now raging inferno with buckets of water from a well. The only mechanical aids they had were stirrup pumps.

Understandably the Trustees of the school were somewhat upset. They lobbied the Town Council and this, together with the general public disquiet led to the Council making the statement that, "everything possible would be done to safeguard the people and property of the town in the future". No doubt the incident influenced the fire committee's decision to replace the old "steamer" with a modern motor fire engine.

The Arrival of The Grenville

Bideford's first motor engine arrived in June of 1927. She was formally named the "Grenville" by the Mayor, Alderman J M Metherell, in a grand ceremony held on the Pill. The 'Grenville' was one of Merryweather & Son's very latest models. She was finished in the classic vermilion with gold coach lining and had polished brass handrails. Shining bright red in the sun she must have looked a very fine vehicle. Thousands of people were there to witness the official naming ceremony because the same day was chosen as the opening of the Kingsley Road, the new road to Northam. It was a bank holiday Monday, June the 6th, 1927 and on that day Bideford held one of its grandest celebrations ever. The new fire engine and her trailer were driven around the Town before a demonstration was given showing her water throwing capabilities. She was, said Mr Hopson, Vice-Chairman of the Bideford, Northam and Appledore Joint Fire Committee, "the best that money could buy". Perhaps that was just as well, for she cost nearly one thousand seven hundred pounds. At least the cost was not borne by Bideford alone, for by now an agreement had now been reached and the expense was shared with Northam and Bideford Urban District Councils. "No longer", continued Mr Hopson, "would the Fire Brigade be laughed and jeered at, being pulled behind a lorry".

The petrol engined Merryweather pumping appliance had two pumps. The 'Hatfield' main pump could shoot 250 gallons per minute at a pressure of 120 pound per square inch. A second Hatfield trailer pump was pulled behind. This positive action pump was man-handled into position and could be got into awkward places where the engine could not. The trailer pump was capable of pumping 150 gallons per minute. It can be seen behind the engine on the picture taken on the Westleigh

21

Straight. (Illustration number 15). The operation and setting up of the pumps required considerable skill and was always in the charge of one man – the Engineer. For many years this was Harry Blackmore. In full the 'Grenville' was manned by a crew of 12. The Corporation and Captain Charles Morris were justly very proud of their new Fire Engine. A new St John's Motor Ambulance had also been bought recently and together the two vehicles were put on show for most of the day. They were, reported the Gazette, "evidence to the visitor, of Bideford and its district, efficiency and enterprise".

With her cast iron wheels and solid rubber tyres providing what must have been a very bumpy ride, the 'Grenville' was to feature very strongly in the history of Bideford and of the Bideford Fire Brigade.

The First Emergency

Indeed she was to see service on that very day. An alarm was raised and Captain Morris had to get word to his men, some of whom were by now watching the spectacular historical pageant that was taking place in the Park. Soon the polished brass bell was sounding its warning and the Brigade proudly raced away; fully under their own steam at last. The fire they were called to deal with was in the loft of a house in Honestone Street and it was successfully brought under control within half an hour. The incident showed that Captain Morris and his Brigade were already fully familiar with their new Engine and equipment. Charles Morris was a plumber and gas-fitter by trade and he joined the Fire Brigade in 1912. His great grandson, Richard

Morris, is able to relate the family story of how Charles came to join the Fire Brigade in the first place. One day Charles was walking home from work with his tools when he was confronted by a band of frightened people running from a shop in Mill Street. A pipe had fractured and the shop was rapidly filling with gas. Charles took command of the situation and went into the shop with his tools and put matters to right there and then. Not long after this the Mayor made a short address of thanks in which he suggested that such a public spirited person should join the Fire Brigade. Charles took his advice and went on to serve with the Bideford Fire Brigade for the next thirty-four years! He became the Captain of the Brigade in 1920 and retired in 1946, when his son Stan, took over. As well as being a local businessman Charles Morris was a keen and successful sportsman being particularly well known in the rowing clubs. He also served as president of the Rotary Club.

The Competitions Continue

From the earliest times the Town and the West of England Fire Brigades used to compete with one another to demonstrate their skills. This practice has continued right up to the present with Fire Brigades competing with one another to prove their efficiency. For many years between the wars the Fire Brigades Association held competitions between the Brigades of the regions to test their speed of turn-out and getting "ready-for-action". Cups and shields were held by the winning Brigade which were suitably inscribed. In typical Bideford style the local Brigade looked forward enthusiastically to these events and often won more than their fair share of the cups and trophies. Clifford Coates remembers that Firemen Jack Mallet and Bill Nicholls were just about the fastest pair around when it came to running out and shinning up a ladder. No doubt their trades as builder, and painter & decorator had a major influence on their performance! Bideford played host to one of the F.B.A. Competitions in 1935 and no fewer than nineteen brigades and about 200 officers and men took part. They competed in seven different competitions for ten trophies, of which Bideford won two, including, of course, first place for the fire escape competition.

The New Fire Station
By now the Fire Station was located on its present site in a building that ironically became available as the result of another major fire. This time it was the Bideford Old Town Boys School that was to be extensively damaged by fire in January of 1926. Fortunately the fire broke out on the weekend and none of the 440 or so boys on the register were in any danger. Unfortunately though, an extensive photographic record of the Bideford boys who served in the first world war was lost in this fire. Not long after, the Brigade took occupancy of the only wing of the building that was still serviceable. The building was temporarily converted to meet their needs, and then, in 1928, it was completely refurbished and customised. It was officially taken over on the 21st of December 1928 by the then conjoined, "Bideford, Northam and District Fire Brigade". Captain Morris was able to demonstrate the opening and closing of the fast acting folding doors and he drove the fire engine out into the street and back again. Photographs were taken to mark the occasion, one of which is still hanging on the wall of the Fire Station (see illustration number 8).

A Second Engine
At the January 1938 meeting of the Bideford Northam and District Joint Fire Brigade Committee it was agreed that anoth-

er new fire engine was needed. It was becoming obvious that the eleven year old "Grenville" was a bit slow on the hills of the district, and rather than to modernise her at a cost of some two to three hundred pounds, it was considered best to buy a new engine. A sum of £1200 was set aside for the purpose.

In the christening ceremony held in the Park in August of 1938, "Kippling" was the name given to the six cylinder Morris Commercial Fire Engine. She could develop 80 horse power and had a modern four speed gear-box. The Merryweather "Hatfield" fire pump could deliver 300 gallons at 200Ib, 350 gallons at 180Ib or 400 gallons at 100Ib per square inch. An added feature was that she could carry the existing wheeled escape ladder that was used with the Grenville. Once again she had woodwork finished in vermilion but this time the trims were lined in silver instead of gold and the panels of the main box doors were lettered, "Bideford Northam and District Joint Fire Committee". The main attraction of this celebration, at least as far as the children were concerned, was a tower that had been erected in the Park. From this tower the children could jump into a sheet held by the firemen. Just to prove he was no spoil-sport the Chief Officer, Charles Morris, also jumped into the sheet. He came down, the newspaper coverage relates, "in a most graceful style".

On a rather more serious note, the opportunity was not missed at this ceremony for the Chief Officer to make an appeal for volunteer auxiliary firemen to come forward and join the Brigade under the new Air Raid Precautions Scheme. Already the Country was gearing herself to the impending war and Bideford men would be sure to play their part.

4. The War Years

During the war Bideford was regarded as a relatively important Fire Brigade Station. Perhaps this was due to the importance of Appledore Shipyard and to the military installations in and around Instow. The number of fire crew more than doubled in the war years. Many of the supplementary men and women who joined the force were on a "green card" from areas such as London. The toll of the London Blitz on Home Counties fire crew was enormous and many were sent to places such as Bideford for a period of recovery. In return many provincial firemen saw service in and around the Capital.

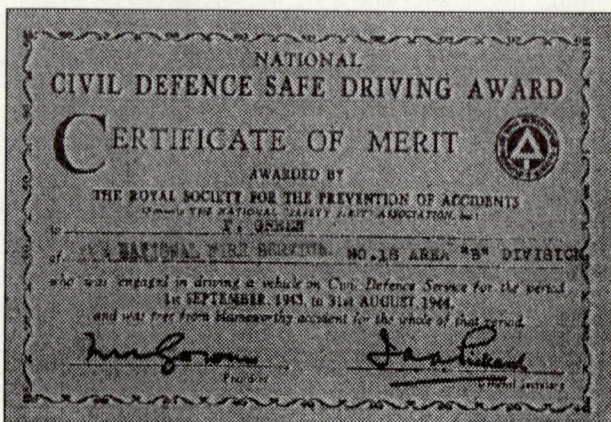

The Civil Defence Safe Driving Certificate awarded to Bideford NFS fireman Trevor Green. (Paula Martin)

In 1938 the Home Office required that an Auxiliary Fire
Service (AFS) was to be formed from local volunteers to aug-
ment the "regular" fire brigade. Although set up before the war
the purpose of the AFS was to assist the fire brigade in the
event of air-raids and to fight fires caused by enemy action.
Despite the institution of the AFS the fire fighting forces of the
country in general were still very piecemeal and uncoordinated.
Bideford was better provided for than most local authorities of
its size, having as it did, both the "Grenville" and "Kippling".
Even so, Chief Officer Morris had to point out in 1940 that his
mens' uniforms were then twenty five years old and in dire
need of replacement. On a national scale the Government
made a serious effort to standardise the fire brigades of the
Country in August of 1941 when it set up the National fire
Service, (NFS). Bideford became 'B' Division of Northern Fire
Force Area 18. Service in the NFS was made compulsory for
some. Chief Officer Charles Morris now became Company
Officer. The influx of new men and equipment meant much
more work for him and his second in command George "Harry"
Blackmore and the rest of the men. They were now responsible
for the training and supervision of the new men in addition to
their normal duties. For a short time at the beginning of the
war, C.O. Morris and three of his firemen were employed on a
full time basis. The Fire Station Tower in Old Town was the
main observation post for the Home Guard and firewatchers
were on duty there from dusk till dawn. Of the four full time
firemen two were put on duty at a time, two manning the station by day and two by night. This was the period of the
"phoney war" however, and the local authorities soon found
that the service was too costly to maintain. The men reverted
back to their retained part-time status after a few months. Not
that Charles Morris minded that. As already stated he was a
plumber by trade and he had a private business to run at the
same time as his fire fighting work. His business was operated
out of his shop on the corner of Abbotsham Road, just along
the road from the Fire Station.

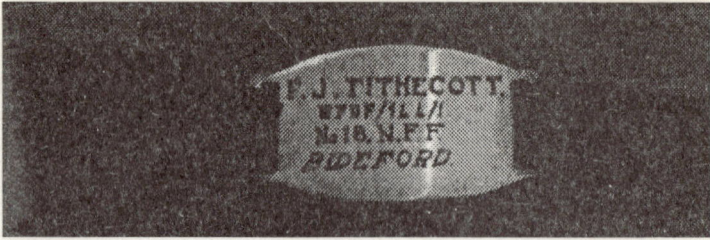

A Second Fire Station

As well as the increase in men at this time there was a corresponding increase in equipment to look after. By 1941 in addition to the two fire engines there were now seven trailer pumps. An additional Fire Station was built in Torrington Street, East-the-Water, in the premises that now belong to Bideford Bicycle Hire. Fire cover could now be provided either side of the river should the bridge be destroyed.

Another minor innovation of the war years was the installation of bells in the homes of the firemen. This was necessary because sirens were only allowed to be used for warning of air-raids. The Council contracted the Bideford Post Office to install the bells so that the alarm could be raised from one call point in the Fire Station and all the firemen of the Town could be summoned at once.

Fortunately there were no major fires due to air raids in the Bideford area during the war but the increased activity and influx of service personnel meant an inevitable increase in accidental fires. In 1940 there was a large fire in the bus depot at Bank End and the store of spare tyres was destroyed. Exploding oil and grease drums added fuel to the fire and danger for the firemen. In September Bideford and District Steam Laundry and W E Gloves Ltd lost their buildings in the largest fire since the one at Edgehill College twenty years before. The Town was lit-up by the fire, one resident claiming that he could read a newspaper by it, three quarters of a mile away. It was the middle of the night and with the blackout in force many people were fearful that the blaze would attract enemy aeroplanes. The building was originally the collar works. Mr J. Boyle of Buckleigh Laundry helped the rival laundry business to survive by taking on some of their work. Little was Mr Boyle to know then, that descendants of his family were to see their business suffer the same fate some 54 years later.

Home Guard HQ Ablaze

On February the 18th 1942 it was the turn of the Head Quarters of the 5th (Bideford) Battalion, Devon Home Guard to catch fire. The Company Stores were kept in rooms at the rear of the Ship Inn that is now "Mr Chips" on the Quay. The entrance was at the side of the building in Conduit Lane. The stores were stacked full of live ammunition with quantities of grenades and explosives as well as the usual clothing and equipment. The outbreak of fire was detected at 6.15 in the evening and by 6.35 p.m. Company Officer Morris and his National Service Firemen were there on the scene. Jack Mallett, in his eightieth year, remembered it well. With hoses playing, the firemen together with officers and men of the Home Guard were doing all they could to both extinguish the fire and at the same time salvage the valuable but potentially lethal stores. Few weapons were destroyed since most had been transferred a few days earlier. Valuable records and files for the first two years of the Bideford Home Guard, however, were lost. Ammunition was going off all around the fire fighters. It took two and a half hours to get the fire under control and pretty soon Allhalland Street was looking like an ammunition dump. There were cases upon cases of live cartridges and hand grenades and armed sentries were posted in the street to guard it. Twice during the night the fire rekindled and it was not until after three in the morning that some firemen were able to leave the scene. Jack Mallett was one among a good number of men that night who performed very brave and gallant action although none, as far as I am aware, received any official recognition.

The very next day a particularly bad fire occurred at Sydney House, Torrington, when five children lost their lives.

The photograph (illustration number 22) is believed to have been taken at this fire with the residential school for delicate children blazing in the background. It was a bitterly cold night and the firemens' efforts were frustrated by water freezing in the pipes. The Grenville can be seen with one hose connected. Reggie Prance the Engineer stands facing, lit by the powerful acetylene lamps of the Grenville. Bill Nicholls and a Torrington man are looking on.

Help For Plymouth and Bristol
The "Grenville" also saw service in South Devon. During 1941 when Plymouth and Devonport were so heavily bombed, men and engines were called from all corners of the South West to help quell the raging fires. Summoned from Bideford the "Grenville" and her crew were there to help. Jack Mallett, once again, recalled that they had the fright of their lives just on the outskirts of Plymouth. As they trundled along in the darkness there was a tremendous explosion just beside them on the edge of the road. Whether it was a time delayed bomb or a land-mine nobody knew, but Jack remembered that they all left the engine pretty quickly. He took shelter in the only available place there seemed to be in the blackness – underneath the fire engine! Later when they got to duty, one of their first calls was to a warehouse fire and Jack remembered cans of Brasso exploding all around them – just like the shells in the home Guard fire. The "Grenville" was said to be the very last mobile unit in action in Plymouth. Not on account of her late arrival, but because of her solid tyres – one by one the pneumatic tyres of the more modern engines burst in the heat and flames.

Unfortunately in July of 1995 Jack Mallett passed away, but before his death he related that the "Grenville" also took her crew to Bristol on a similar mission of assistance after a blitz. The old and slow engine made staying on board difficult enough, but after the long and uncomfortable journey they arrived in the black of night in a very thick fog. The crew had to lead the engine along the road, straining their eyes in the darkness to pick out the verge at the side of the road with torches. Jack mostly remembered being absolutely exhausted by the time they made the city.

Tragic Accident

Although she featured quite strongly in the affections of the people of Bideford and the Brigade in particular, not all incidents relating to the "Grenville" were happy ones. Late in 1940 after attending a fire in Northam, she was involved in a fatal accident in Mill Street. Whenever the brightly coloured engine with her long escape ladder was spotted, the children of Bideford were attracted to it like moths to a flame. On this occasion tragedy struck and an eleven year old boy, Wallace Cawsey, was run over. A number of children had climbed on to the engine when it stopped in Mill Street for one of the firemen to go into a shop. When the engine pulled away again Wallace was a bit slow in jumping off. When he finally jumped from the side-box he lost his balance and stumbled back from the edge of the pavement. He fell under one of the solid back wheels of the engine which went over him. He died later in hospital. In a subsequent enquiry Frank Passmore, the driver, was absolved of any blame.

Bomber Crash

The closest Bideford came to having a really major war-time disaster was when an armed Wellington bomber crashed into wasteland at East-the-Water on March 10th 1945. The Royal Canadian Air Force aeroplane was on a routine homing flight and had taken off from Chivenor just four minutes earlier. Codenamed 'P' for Peter, the plane developed an engine fault and failed to gain height. Coming down lower and lower over the river it cleared Bideford's ancient bridge only to smash into "Roundhill" on the east bank. Whether by chance or the determined effort of the pilot the aircraft narrowly missed the gasworks, the electricity station and the densely populated area

around Clifton Street. The tip of one of the wings actually
struck the retort building of the gas-works. Of the full crew of
four there was only one survivor. It was about 8.15 on a
Wednesday evening and one of the first civilians on the scene
was Gas Company worker Walter Johns of Clifton Street. He
was later awarded the British Empire Medal for his efforts in
helping to rescue the rear gunner from the burning fuselage.
Unfortunately the airman was to die of his injuries later.

Soon the wreckage was blazing fiercely with ammunition,
fuel and flares adding to the danger. Both full-time and part-
time members of the National Fire Service from Bideford,
Instow and Appledore were called to help Company Officer
Morris and his men tackle the potentially disastrous blaze.
Nearly 4000 feet of hose was used with three trailer pumps in
action. Although three Canadian airmen lost their lives in this
incident the toll in civilian casualties could have been very
much higher. The death of the airmen was commemorated in a
remembrance service held in Bideford on March 12th 1995
when a number of Canadian ex-service men attended.

"The Good Hope"
A familiar sight on the river in the war years was the Bideford
NFS fire barge the "Good Hope". She was usually moored in
Bideford Pool, by the Long Bridge, and was in the charge of
Leading Fireman Arthur Pridham. Two other NFS firemen
made up the crew. The boat was a converted rowing lifeboat
formerly belonging to the Royal National Lifeboat Institution at
Ilfracombe. The "Good Hope" was famous for being the first
and only jet-propelled fire barge that belonged to the National
Fire Service. Arthur Pridham and a team of local helpers fitted
two standard NFS pumps to the vessel. One of these was used
to propel the barge by pumping water to any of four jets just
below the water line, either at the stern or at the bow. She had
a speed of about six knots and was extremely manoeuvrable.
Fortunately she was not called upon to prove her capabilities in
any real emergency, but she was frequently used to pump water

through the system of pipes that were laid in the streets of Bideford at this time. River water was thus got to the higher parts of the Town and stored ready for use in any emergency – a practice that had originated hundreds of years earlier.

5. Recent Years

From its formation in 1941 to the end of April 1945 the brigades of the North Devon Fire Force Area had attended no fewer than 1100 fires. After the war Bideford retained some of the ex Auxiliary and National Fire Service vehicles it had gained during the war. These were the "ATVs" or Auxiliary Towing Vehicles with towed "Major" pumps and "Sultzer" heavy pumping appliances. Costly lessons had been learned during the war, especially with regard to the non-compatibility of equipment, but these problems were now largely overcome. In 1948 the NFS was disbanded although the AFS was reinstated and lasted for a few more years. Control of fire fighting services was now given to the county authorities, and Devon County Fire Service was created. Bideford became Station B9.

Fred Tithecott succeeded Stan Morris as Chief Officer of the Bideford Station in 1949. Fred is alive and well today and in his 82nd year. Before his retirement he was a well-known local builder as well as being a past president and captain of the Bowling Club. Fred's main memory of his fire service was when he spent four days helping with the flood relief work after the Lynmouth disaster in 1952. About fifty volunteer firemen were on duty at any one time and they came from all over the county.

When Fred retired in 1961 his position was taken over by Sub Officer Tom Trick. Tom assumed full responsibility on his promotion to Chief Officer in 1964. The last major fire Tom attended was that of the Atlanta Hotel in Westward Ho! which was somewhat ironic in that he had helped to decorate it when it was first built as "Dormy House" years earlier. Tom retired in 1970 and is still alive and well and living in Northam. His son Arthur was a full-time fireman at Ilfracombe and so was another grandson, Chris Bridgeman. The tradition of the fireman lives on in the blood!

Clifford Coates took over from Tom as Chief Officer in 1970 and the reader is referred to the introduction.

"Fire-fighters"
Since the war the role of the Fireman has changed considerably and so too has their title. "Fire-fighter" is the title used today and it more aptly describes their roll as well as helping to encompass the growing number of women who now join the fire and rescue service. These days there is an increasing proportion of calls not just to fires but to render assistance and rescue at accidents. This widening of the service was recognised in 1986 when the name "Devon County Fire Brigade"

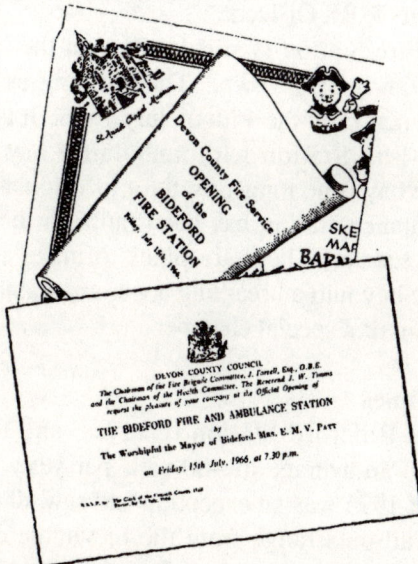

The invitation to Ted & Joyce Webb from Devon County Council to the opening of Bideford Fire Brigade and Ambulance Station, 15th July, 1966. In the background can be seen detail of a knapkin designed by John Dyke to commemorate the event for the Three Bears' of Barnstaple who did the catering.

was changed to "Devon Fire and Rescue Service".

The present Headquarters of the Devon Fire and Rescue Service is at Clyst St George, on the outskirts of Exeter. The County is split into nine districts each named after a river in their locality. The Taw District (Barnstaple), and the Torridge District (Bideford), being prime examples. There are fifty eight stations in total, of which seven are manned on a full-time basis; four are day manned/retained; and forty-six retained manned; and one that is volunteer manned.

Station 04 (Bideford), is a retained Station under the control of Station Officer Graham Tucker. He has two sub Officers, three Leading Fire-fighters and fourteen Fire-fighters. The station also houses the District Offices for Torridge which covers stations at Appledore, Chumleigh, Hartland, Torrington and Witheridge as well as Bideford. The District Officer is Assistant Divisional Officer Bob Prince, GI Fire E. His support Officer is Station Officer Dave Turner. Both of these men are full-time DF & RS Officers.

The Fire Station is still located on the land that it took over in 1926 in Old Town. The building as it is today was officially opened on the 15th of July 1966. It is a purpose-built three bay Fire Station with ambulance bay attached. The ambulance bay is no longer used for its original purpose since a new ambulance station has been built on the Clovelly Road Industrial Estate. There are plans to make a part of the old ambulance bay into a breathing apparatus training area with the construction of a special chamber.

Present Times

Today the Bideford Station receives, and the fire-fighters respond, to an average of 400 calls per year. The hot and dry summer of 1995 was an exception and saw all previous records broken. Call-outs range from the inevitable chimney fires to major multi-pump fires, and from road traffic accidents to floods.

Modern fire-fighters have to be familiar with a varied

assortment of technical equipment and apparatus and they have to be aware of a vast number of potentially dangerous chemicals and substances. Just recently Bideford fire-fighters had to tackle a fire in a disused warehouse that contained no fewer than 96 drums of leaking chemicals. Among these were drums of cyanide, acids and alkalis. Fire-fighters have to have a knowledge of the construction of buildings as they are often at risk from falling masonry or from falling through fire weakened floors.

Recent large and dangerous fires in the area have included those of Buckleigh Laundry, Westward Ho! and Scudders Emporium in Bridge Street.

The Buckleigh Laundry fire illustrates that even with a very prompt response and the latest modern appliances a fire can still get the upper hand for a time. Eighty-six fire-fighters were involved in this fire with six jets and eight sets of breathing apparatus. Glass from the roof-lights and bulbs melted. The Bideford crew were the first on the scene arriving within *six minutes* of the alarm being raised at around midnight.

Scudder's fire involved over fifty firemen from six stations, the network of rooms, basements and corridors making the fire particularly difficult to control. This time there were sleeping people in the flats above and one newspaper report rightly described the work of the fire-fighters at this fire as "heroic".

Whenever they respond to a call the fire-fighters can never be quite sure what they are going to find or what they will need to do. The list of qualities and skills required of a good fire-fighter – both past and present – is long and very comprehensive. Retained fire-fighters are on call twenty-four hours a day and they must be prepared to drop whatever they are doing to report immediately to the station. They are required to attend training drill and practices on a regular basis and must be prepared to attend the occasional course to keep up to date with the latest technology. The inhabitants of Bideford are very fortunate that there is no shortage of suitable volunteers. From the very start the loyalty and dedication of the men of "The Fire Brigade" has been reflected in these pages. In the past many local men have given a great deal of their time and effort for periods over a great many years, often in succeeding generations. Today the tradition continues. And long may it do so!

APPENDIX 1.

Chronology and Captains of the Brigade

1851   William Major, Town.

Mr Hamlyn, West of England.

1858   William Major, Town.

E M White, Inspector. John Abbot, Engineer.
Mr R E Yelland, Representative, West of England
Fire Brigade.

1870   William Major, Superintendent, Fire Engine Station,
Town Hall.

E M White, Superintendent. William Way of North
Street, Foreman. .
John Abbot, Engineer, West of England Fire Engine
Station, The Strand.

1878   John Abbot, Superintendent. William Way, Foreman,
West of England Fire Brigade Service, The Quay.

1887   Directive to form new Town Fire Brigade.
Henry Chowins Captain, 3 River View Terrace.
Borough Surveyor.

1892   Henry Chowins, Captain of Brigade, 6 Cooper Street,
(where the keys were kept).
The Town Fire Brigade Station, Broad Quay.
(just below Cooper Street).

1903   Henry Chowins retires after 16 years.
        Frederick Lee of Wellbrook Terrace replaces him.
        The keys now kept at No 2 Allhalland Street.
        Second hand-cart stored in the Market.
        (Honey's the Butchers' Shop).

1920   Frederick Lee retires.
        Charles Morris of Abbotsham Road made Captain.

1923   Fire Station, Market Square.
        Charles Morris Captain.
        Alarm bell now at the top of High Street.
        Steam fire engine attends fire, Jan 1923.

1926   Charles Morris, the Brigade Station, the Pannier Market
        (Tel. The Police, Bideford 40).
        Partial move of the Fire Brigade Station to its present
        site in Old Town.

1946   Charles Morris retires after 34 years service, 26 as
        Chief Officer.
        His son Stan Morris succeeds him until 1949.

1949 to 1961   Fred Tithecott.

1961 to 1964   Cover by Tom Trick as Sub Officer.

1964 to 1970   Tom Trick

1970 to 1979   Clifford Coates

1979 to 1981   Kenny Upton

1981   Graham Tucker

Some Notable Dates

1852 December, Southcott Farm fire

1866 June, Hyfield House fire

1871 "Fire-Plugs" fitted throughout the Town.

1885 March, Apps Brewery fire.

1888 National Fire Brigades union formed in London

1891 February, first major fire of new Brigade: Kivell's
      Coach Works.

1920 June, Edgehill College fire.

1914 Fire Station moved to the Market Square.

1917 Steam Fire Engine purchased (believed).

1916 January, Old Town School fire.

1927 Formation of the Bideford, Northam and District Joint
      Fire Service. First motor fire engine, the "Grenville".

1928 December, official opening of "joint" fire station, Old
      Town. (As late as 1932 there is still reference to
      equipment in the old fire station in the Market Place).

1940 September, Bideford and District Steam Laundry Fire.

1938 Auxiliary Fire Service instituted

1941	National Fire Service formed
1942	February, Home Guard HQ fire
1945	March, RCAF Wellington Bomber crash
1948	Devon County Fire Service formed
1966	July, present Fire Station opened, Old Town
1974	Change of name to Devon Fire Brigade
1986	Change of name to Devon Fire and Rescue Service
1994	February, Buckleigh Laundry fire

APPENDIX 2

Appliances of the Bideford Brigade

Dates of registration and when disposed of.

1927 to –   Merryweather pump-escape.   (UO 2879)

1938 to 1962   Morris/Merryweather/Braidwood pump
                escape. (EUO 881)

1952 to 1976   Dennis F8, water tender ladder, converted from
                water tender. (OTA 966)

1967 to 1982   Bedford J5, water tender.   (KDV 958F)

1971 to 1985   Bedford, water tender ladder, subsequently
                converted to multi-purpose appliance.
                (UUO 433J)

1978 to –   Dennis D, multi-purpose water tender ladder.
                (XTT 307S)

1989 to –   Volvo FL6, water tender ladder.   (G79 OTA)

SOURCES

Mainly newspaper researches from The Bideford and North Devon Gazette and the North Devon Journal. Other sources include :

A Concise History of Bideford. Inkerman Rogers.

Devon at War. Gerald Wasley.

Edgehill College 1884-1934. Richard Pyke.

Fire Appliances of Devon. Roy W Yeoman.

Fire Engines and Fire Fighting. David Burgess-Wise

Fire Fighting for the A F S. G W Underdown

History of Bideford. Reverend Roger Granville, M.A.

History of the 5th (Bideford) Battalion Devon Home Guard. Colonel DC Crombie

Links with the Past (The Eagle Insurance Co.) AF Shepherd

Old Bideford and District. Murial Goaman.

The Book of Bideford. Alison Grant and Peter Christie.

READERS NOTES